Copyright © 2019 by Learning with Harmony, LLC.
www.learningwithharmony.com
Book Cover & Illustrations Designed by Aranahaj Iqbal

All rights reserved. No part of this book may be reproduced or transmitted in any form or by any means, electronic or mechanical, including photocopying, recording, or by any information storage and retrieval system, without permission in writing from the author.

ISBN: 978-1-948398-12-1

About the Author

LaTonya D. Steele has spent 20+ years of her career teaching high school and adult learners business courses in the community college system. She is a firm believer that a good education is essential for all ages. She has a passion for giving back to others and helping them succeed in reaching their academic, professional, and personal goals. LaTonya has a Ph.D. in Management and is a lifelong learner.

Since the birth of her first granddaughter, LaTonya has recently developed a new interest in writing educational books for children. She started writing books for her granddaughter and wanted to share them with other children, families, caregivers, and early childhood educators. LaTonya decided to make an educational book series (**Learning with Harmony**) for children from birth to 4 years old. The main characters in the book are her granddaughter Harmony and dog Penny. You can visit her website at www.learningwithharmony.com.

About the Illustrator

Aranahaj Iqbal has been illustrating for over six years and has many published books. She enjoys illustrating children's books. She also provides illustrations for book series, single books, and long-term projects. You can visit her Facebook page at facebook.com/aranahajart, Instagram at aranahajiqbal and Twitter at Aranahaji (ARANAHAHJI) to see her portfolios.

Learning the Alphabet with Harmony

Written By LaTonya D. Steele   Illustrated By Aranahaj Iqbal

Hi! I am Harmony and I want you to learn the alphabet with me! We will have lots of fun learning with Penny and my friends.

Aa

act

Abbey likes to act like a frog. Do you know how to act like a frog?

Bb

build

Brandon likes to build a house with blocks.
What do you like to build?

Cc

crawl

Carley can crawl fast. Do you know how to crawl?

Dd

drink

Dashon likes to drink milk. What do you like to drink?

Ee

eat

Erica likes to eat eggs. What do you like to eat?

Ff

flip

Fatima likes to flip upside down. Do you know how to flip?

Gg

grow

Grayson planted seeds that will grow into flowers. Do you like to watch the flowers grow?

Hh

hear

Harmony can hear Penny barking. What sounds do you hear?

Ii

inspect

Isabel inspects her room to make sure it is clean. Do you inspect your room?

Jj

jump

Jose can jump high. How high can you jump?

Kk

kick

Kendra can kick the ball far. Do you know how to kick a ball?

Ll

look

LaShonda likes to look out of the window. What do you see when you look out of the window?

Mm

make

Macie likes to make cookies with her mom.
What do you like to make in the kitchen?

Nn

nap

Nick is taking a nap. Do you like to take a nap?

Oo

open

Omar can open the door. Can you open a door?

Pp

play

Penny likes to play outside in the rain. Do you like to play in the rain?

Qq

quiet

Quinton is quiet. Can you be very quiet?

Rr

run

Remmi can run fast. Can you run fast?

Ss

see

Sammie can see the bright stars at night.
What do you see at night in the sky?

Tt

talk

Trent likes to talk about trucks. Do you like to talk about trucks?

Uu

under

Ursula is hiding under the blanket. Where do you like to hide?

Vv

visit

Vicky likes to visit her grandma. Do you visit your grandma?

Ww

walk

Wendy likes to walk to school. Where do you like to walk?

Xx

X-ray

Xavier goes to the doctor for an X-ray. Can you see his bones?

Yy

yell

Yoshi can yell very loud. How loud can you yell?

Zz

zip

Zoie can zip up her coat. Can you zip up your coat?

I like learning the alphabet. Practice reading the alphabet with me.

Aa Bb Cc Dd Ee
Ff Gg Hh Ii Jj Kk
Ll Mm Nn Oo Pp
Qq Rr Ss Tt Uu
Vv Ww Xx Yy Zz